Guitar Songs for Little Rockers

Wrriten by — Dr. Hoot

Published in 2025 by Skooler Books

Guitar Songs for Little Rockers

Skooler Books

ISBN: 9789355251947

Songs

Muffin Man

For He's a Jolly Good Fellow

Hot Cross Buns

Little Miss Muffet

Hickory Dickory Dock

Jingle Bells

A Tisket A Tasket

Old MacDonald Had a Farm

Baa Baa Black Sheep

My Bonnie Lies Over the Ocean

Yankee Doodle

Pat-a-Cake

Little Boy Blue

Muffin Man

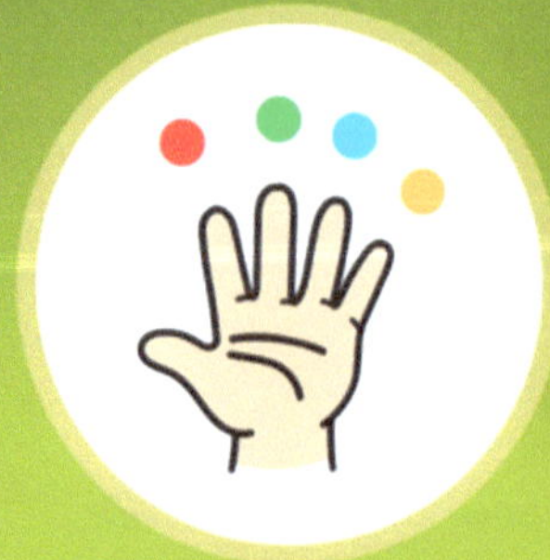

Strumming

↓ ↓ ↓ ↑

D
Oh, do you know the muffin man,

G A7
The muffin man, the muffin man?

D
Do you know the muffin man

G A7
Who lives on Drury Lane?

D
Yes, I know the muffin man,

G A7
The muffin man, the muffin man.

D
Yes, I know the muffin man

G A7
Who lives on Drury Lane.

For He's a Jolly Good Fellow

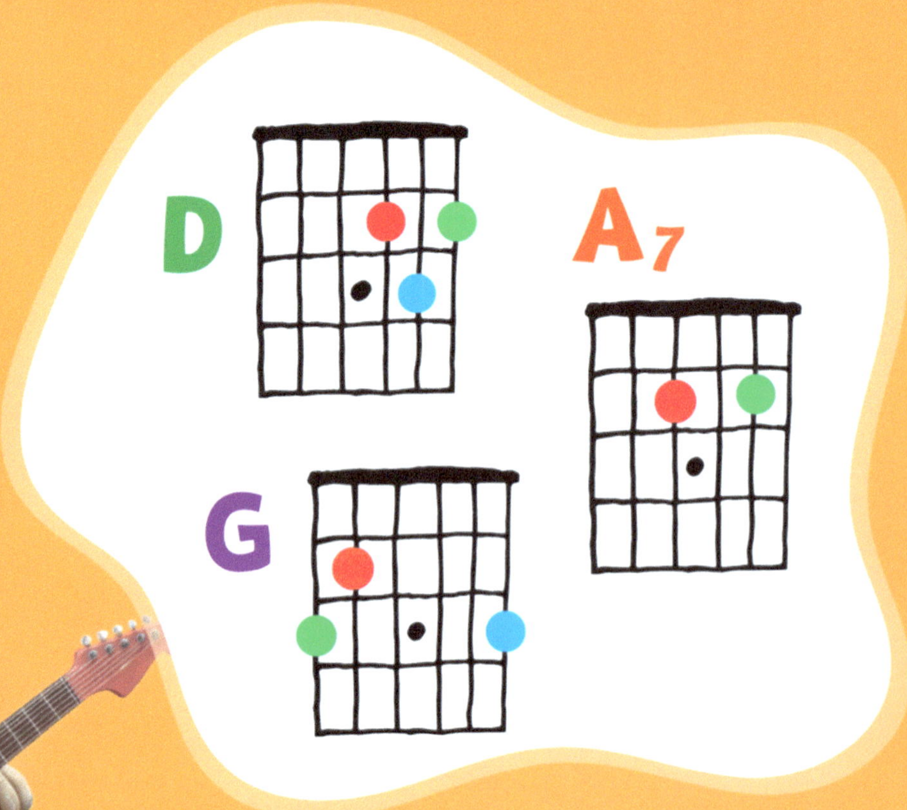

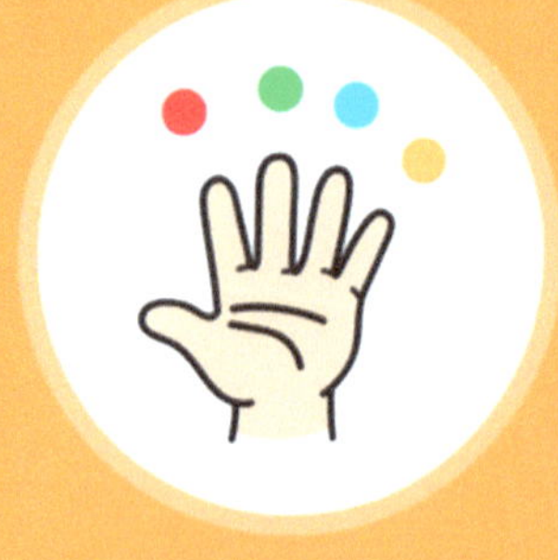

Strumming

```
D
For he's a jolly good fellow,
G               D
For he's a jolly good fellow,
D               A7
For he's a jolly good fellow,
  A7                  D
  Which nobody can deny!
  D                   A7
  Which nobody can deny,
  A7                  D
  Which nobody can deny,
D               A7
For he's a jolly good fellow,
  A7                  D
  Which nobody can deny!
```

Jingle Bells

Strumming

↓ ↓ ↓ ↑

C
Dashing through the snow,

C G
in a one-horse open sleigh

G D7
Over the fields we go,

D7 G
Laughing all the way.

G
Jingle bells, jingle bells,

G
Jingle all the way!

C
Oh, what fun it is to ride

D7 G
in a one-horse open sleigh.

Hot Cross Buns

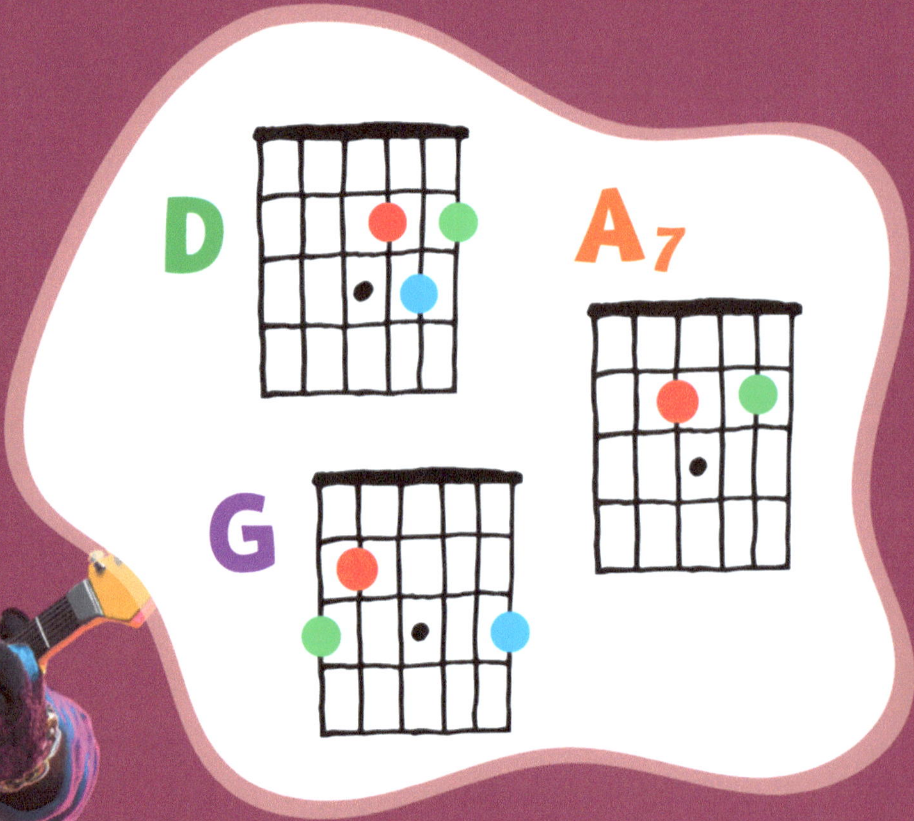

Strumming

↓ ↓ ↓ ↑

D G D
Hot cross buns! Hot cross buns!

A7 D
One a penny, two a penny,

G D
Hot cross buns!

D
If you have no daughters,

G D
Give them to your sons.

A7 D
One a penny, two a penny,

G D
Hot cross buns!

A Tisket A Tasket

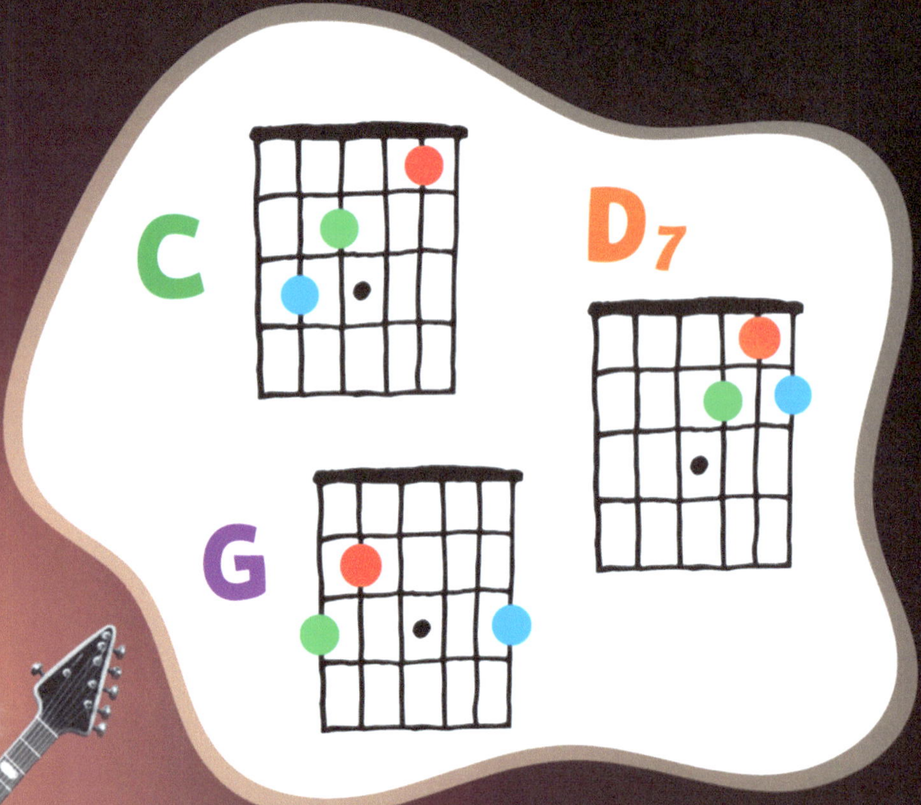

Strumming

↓ ↓ ↓ ↑

G
A-tisket, a-tasket,

C
a green and yellow basket.

G
I wrote a letter to my love,

D7
And on the way I dropped it.

G
I dropped it, I dropped it,

C
And on the way I dropped it.

G
A little boy he picked it up

D7 G
And put it in his pocket.

Old MacDonald Had a Farm

Strumming

↓ ↓ ↓ ↑

G D
Old MacDonald had a farm, E-I-E-I-O!

G D
And on his farm he had a cow, E-I-E-I-O!

C
With a moo-moo here,

G
And a moo-moo there,

C
Here a moo, there a moo,

G
Everywhere a moo-moo!

Baa Baa Black Sheep

Strumming

↓ ↓ ↓ ↑

```
G
Baa, baa, black sheep,
C                   G
Have you any wool?
C                     D
Yes sir, yes sir, Three bags full.
G
One for the master,
C
One for the dame,
G
And one for the little boy
G                          D
Who lives down the lane.
```

My Bonnie Lies Over the Ocean

Strumming O

↓ ↓ ↓ ↑

D A
My Bonnie lies over the ocean,

D A
My Bonnie lies over the sea,

D A
My Bonnie lies over the ocean,

G D
Oh, bring back my Bonnie to me.

G D
Bring back, bring back,

A D
Oh, bring back my Bonnie to me, to me;

G D
Bring back, bring back,

A D
Oh, bring back my Bonnie to me.

Little Miss Muffet

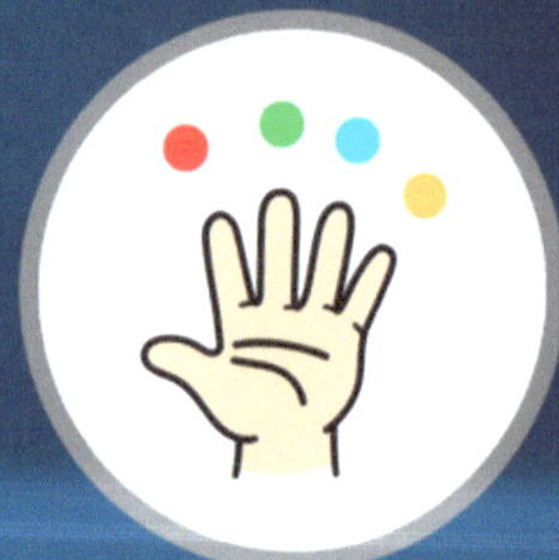

Strumming O

↓ ↓ ↓ ↑

C
Little Miss Muffet

G
sat on a tuffet,

C Am
Eating her curds and whey;

C
Along came a spider,

G
who sat down beside her

C Am
And frightened Miss Muffet away.

Hickory Dickory Dock

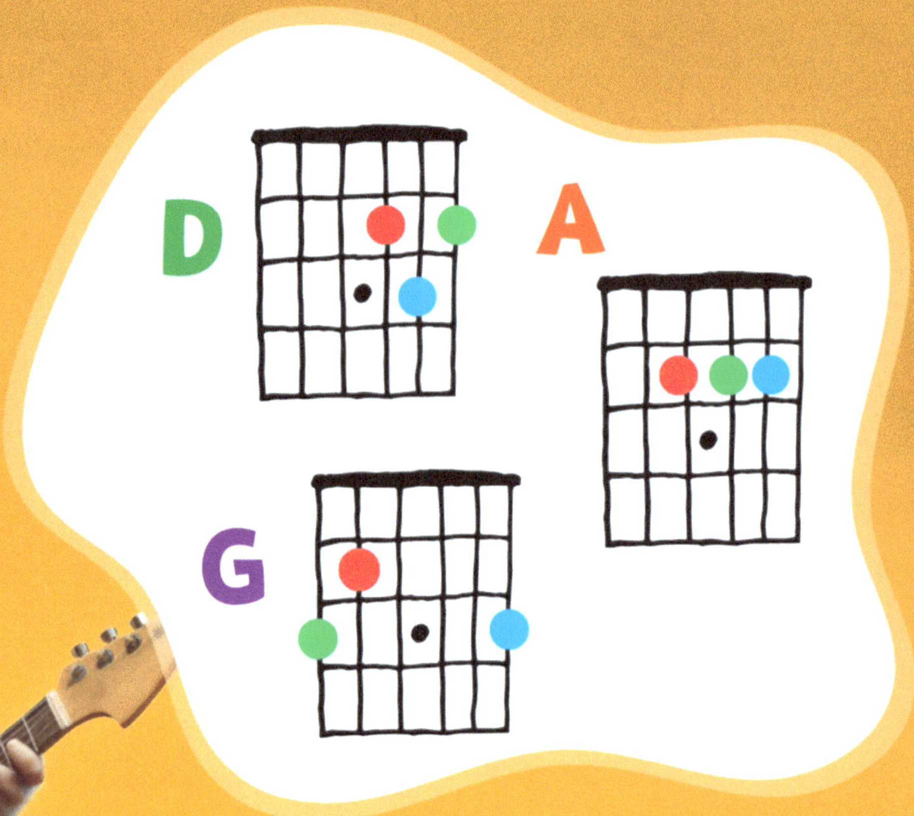

Strumming

↓ ↓ ↓ ↑

D
Hickory dickory dock,

D
The mouse ran up the clock.

G
The clock struck one,

D
The mouse ran down,

A D
Hickory dickory dock,

D
Tick-tock, tick-tock.

Yankee Doodle

Strumming O

↓ ↓ ↓ ↑

G D7
Yankee Doodle went to town,

G C
Riding on a pony;

G D7
Stuck a feather in his cap

G C
And called it macaroni.

C
Yankee Doodle, keep it up,

G
Yankee Doodle dandy;

C
Mind the music and the step,

G C
And with the girls be handy.

Pat-a-Cake

Strumming

↓ ↓ ↓ ↑

D G
Pat-a-cake, pat-a-cake, baker's man,

A7 D
Bake me a cake as fast as you can;

G D
Pat it and prick it and mark it with B,

A7 D
And put it in the oven for baby and me.

D G
Roll it and toss it, Make it a nice one,

A7 D
Stir it and bake it, And serve it for fun.

Little Boy Blue

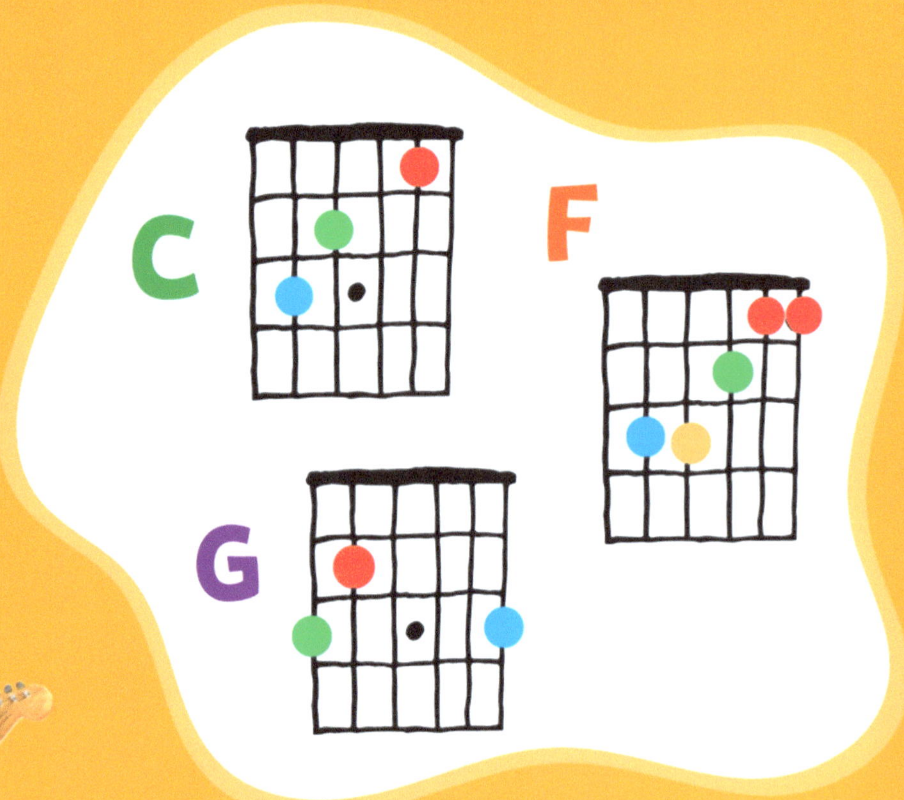

Strumming

↓ ↓ ↓ ↑

C G
Little Boy Blue, come blow your horn.

C
The sheep's in the meadow,

G
the cow's in the corn.

F C
Where is the boy who looks after the sheep?

F G
Under a haystack, fast asleep.

C G
Will you wake him? No, not I,

F G C
For if I do, he will surely cry.

More Book's in the Series

www.ingramcontent.com/pod-product-compliance
Ingram Content Group UK Ltd.
Pitfield, Milton Keynes, MK11 3LW, UK
UKHW061433190726
13845UKWH00021B/168
* 9 7 8 9 3 5 5 2 5 1 9 4 7 *